Instant Spring for Android Starter

Leverage Spring for Android to create RESTful and OAuth Android apps

Anthony Dahanne

PUBLISHING

BIRMINGHAM - MUMBAI

Instant Spring for Android Starter

First published: January 2013

Production Reference: 1220113

Published by Packt Publishing Ltd.
Livery Place
35 Livery Street
Birmingham B3 2PB, UK.

ISBN 978-1-78216-190-5

www.packtpub.com

Credits

Author

Anthony Dahanne

Reviewer

Stanojko Markovik

Acquisition Editor

Usha Iyer

Commissioning Editor

Ameya Sawant

Technical Editor

Jalasha D'costa

Project Coordinator

Michelle Quadros

Proofreader

Lesley Harrison

Production Coordinator

Melwyn D'sa

Conidon Miranda

Cover Work

Conidon Miranda

Cover Image

Conidon Miranda

About the Author

Anthony Dahanne is a Java software developer since 2005. His favorite topics include Android, Continuous Integration, Web Services, and of course, core Java development.

During his spare time, he enjoys hacking on some open source Android app (G2Android, ReGalAndroid, and so on). He also contributes from time to time to build/IDE plugins usually involving Maven and Eclipse.

You can meet him at one of the many Java-related user group gatherings at Montréal (Android Montréal, Montréal JUG, Big Data Montréal, and so on).

Working at Terracotta, he's currently implementing the REST management tools for EhCache.

I would like to thank Guilhem De Miollis for his time spent reviewing the content of the book and even suggesting some topics. My colleagues at the Interfaces team at Terracotta, for always taking the time to share their deep Java knowledge with me, and finally my beloved wife Isabelle for her patience and help to make this book happen.

About the Reviewer

Stanojko Markovik was born in Skopje, Macedonia, but now resides in Paris, France. He holds a master's degree in software engineering from the faculty of electrical engineering and information technologies in his hometown of Skopje. His expertise spans from developing enterprise-level applications; serving millions of clients to developing single-user applications for mobile or desktop using various technologies.

Throughout his career he worked for companies that range from 5 – 10 to 500 – 1000 employees. As an engineer, he is versatile in multiple platforms and technologies including Java, Android, Blackberry, Spring, J2EE, C, and C++.

He has also presented his work at industry conferences on innovative technologies and worked on EU projects to improve the technological advancements of the twenty-first century.

www.PacktPub.com

Support files, eBooks, discount offers and more

You might want to visit www.PacktPub.com for support files and downloads related to your book.

Did you know that Packt offers eBook versions of every book published, with PDF and ePub files available? You can upgrade to the eBook version at www.PacktPub.com and as a print book customer, you are entitled to a discount on the eBook copy. Get in touch with us at service@packtpub.com for more details.

At www.PacktPub.com, you can also read a collection of free technical articles, sign up for a range of free newsletters and receive exclusive discounts and offers on Packt books and eBooks.

PacktLib.PacktPub.com

Do you need instant solutions to your IT questions? PacktLib is Packt's online digital book library. Here, you can access, read and search across Packt's entire library of books.

Why Subscribe?

- ✦ Fully searchable across every book published by Packt
- ✦ Copy and paste, print and bookmark content
- ✦ On demand and accessible via web browser

Free Access for Packt account holders

If you have an account with Packt at www.PacktPub.com, you can use this to access PacktLib today and view nine entirely free books. Simply use your login credentials for immediate access.

Table of Contents

Instant Spring for Android Starter   **1**

So, what is Spring for Android?   **3**
  RestTemplate   3
  Auth/Spring Social   3
  What Spring for Android is not   4
Integrating it in an Android app   **5**
  Minimal dependencies to add or use RestTemplate   5
  Getting started with Eclipse and Spring for Android   5
    Installing the ADT plugin   6
    First example app   9
  Using Maven to build a Spring for Android app   16
Quick start – RestTemplate   **20**
  Different message converters   20
    MappingJacksonHttpMessageConverter   20
    SimpleXmlHttpMessageConverter   22
    RssChannelHttpMessageConverter   25
  Gzip encryption   27
  HTTP Basic authentication   29
  The RESTful recipe app   31
    RecipeList activity: listing all recipes stored on the server   32
    RecipeEditor activity   36
  Android annotations   39
Quick start – OAuth   **42**
  Developing a website or an app relying on a service provider   42
  The OAuth dance   43
  Spring for Android Auth module   45
  An OAuth example using Google   46

People and places you should get to know   **58**

  Official sites   58

  Articles and tutorials   58

  Community   58

  Blogs   58

  Twitter   58

Instant Spring for Android Starter

Welcome to *Instant Spring for Android Starter*. This book has been specially created to provide you with all the information that you need to ease your Android development using Spring for Android. You will learn the different features provided by Spring for Android and get started with building your first apps using these features.

This book contains the following sections:

So, what is Spring for Android? describes Spring for Android has an extension of the Spring Framework that helps simplify the development of native Android applications; it currently (Version 1.o.o.RELEASE) features a REST client (RestTemplate) and OAuth support (Spring Social).

Integrating it in an Android app teaches how to integrate Spring for Android with the Eclipse IDE and ADT (Android Development Tools), as well as with Maven.

Quick start – Rest Template will show you how to use some of the core features of the Spring for Android Rest Template module; for example, creating a REST client. By the end of this section you will be able to retrieve, update, create, and delete REST resources using message converters and/or HTTP Basic authentication.

Quick start – OAuth will show you how to use some of the core features of Spring for Android Auth module; for example, creating an OAuth connection to Google+ to read a user profile. By the end of this section you will be able to establish an OAuth connection to authenticate your user and app.

People and places you should get to know – Every open source project is centered around a community. This section provides you with many useful links to the project page and forums, as well as a number of helpful articles, tutorials and blogs, in addition to the Twitter feeds of Spring for Android super-contributors.

So, what is Spring for Android?

In this first section, we will go through the main aspects of Spring for Android: `RestTemplate`, `Auth`, and what Spring for Android is not.

RestTemplate

The `RestTemplate` module is a port of the Java-based REST client `RestTemplate`, which initially appeared in 2009 in Spring for MVC. Like the other Spring template counterparts (`JdbcTemplate`, `JmsTemplate`, and so on), its aim is to bring to Java developers (and thus Android developers) a high-level abstraction of lower-level Java API; in this case, it eases the development of HTTP clients.

In its Android version, `RestTemplate` relies on the core Java HTTP facilities (`HttpURLConnection`) or the Apache HTTP Client. According to the Android device version you use to run your app, `RestTemplate` for Android can pick the most appropriate one for you. This is according to Android developers' recommendations.

 See `http://android-developers.blogspot.ca/2011/09/androids-http-clients.html`. This blog post explains why in certain cases Apache HTTP Client is preferred over `HttpURLConnection`.

`RestTemplate` for Android also supports gzip compression and different message converters to convert your Java objects from and to JSON, XML, and so on.

Auth/Spring Social

The goal of the Spring Android `Auth` module is to let an Android app gain authorization to a web service provider using **OAuth** (Version 1 or 2).

OAuth is probably the most popular authorization protocol (and it is worth mentioning that, it is an open standard) and is currently used by Facebook, Twitter, Google apps (and many others) to let third-party applications access users account.

Spring for Android `Auth` module is based on several Spring libraries because it needs to securely (with cryptography) persist (via JDBC) a token obtained via HTTP; here is a list of the needed libraries for OAuth:

+ **Spring Security Crypto**: To encrypt the token
+ **Spring Android OAuth**: This extends `Spring Security Crypto` adding a dedicated encryptor for Android, and SQLite based persistence provider
+ **Spring Android Rest Template**: To interact with the HTTP services
+ **Spring Social Core**: The OAuth workflow abstraction

While performing the OAuth workflow, we will also need the browser to take the user to the service provider authentication page, for example, the following is the Twitter OAuth authentication dialog:

What Spring for Android is not

SpringSource (the company behind Spring for Android) is very famous among Java developers. Their most popular product is the Spring Framework for Java which includes a dependency injection framework (also called an inversion of control framework). Spring for Android does not bring inversion of control to the Android platform.

In its very first release (1.0.0.M1), Spring for Android brought a common logging facade for Android; the authors removed it in the next version.

Integrating it in an Android app

Spring for Android is contained in multiple JAR libraries which should be linked to the project. These JAR libraries are not part of the standard Android distribution. For example, we will need the following JAR libraries to consume a JSON REST API with Spring For Android `RestTemplate`:

> ▶ ⟨010⟩ spring-android-rest-template-1.0.0.RELEASE.jar
> ▶ ⟨010⟩ spring-android-core-1.0.0.RELEASE.jar – /Users,
> ▶ ⟨010⟩ jackson-mapper-asl-1.9.7.jar – /Users/anthony,
> ▶ ⟨010⟩ jackson-core-asl-1.9.7.jar – /Users/anthony/.m

Minimal dependencies to add or use RestTemplate

You can use the IDE to manually satisfy the dependencies (and their transitive dependencies). The alternative to manual dependency management is automatic project building with **Maven**. We will explain Maven building later in the section.

Getting started with Eclipse and Spring for Android

Eclipse is certainly the most popular IDE to develop Android apps; one of the reasons why it is so is because the **Android Development Tools** (**ADT**), maintained by Google, provides the Eclipse plugins to ease Android development (debugger, custom XML editors, and so on).

 IntelliJ IDEA Community Edition provides out of the box support for Android; Netbeans also lets you install the `nbandroid` plugin which facilitates Android apps development.

We need to perform the following steps to get started with Eclipse:

1. Download a recent version from `http://www.eclipse.org/downloads` (ADT is compatible with Eclipse from the Version 3.6.2; at the time of writing, 4.2 Juno was the most recent). Prefer *Eclipse IDE for Java developers* rather than the other versions available.

2. Once you have it downloaded and unpacked on your machine, start it. Choose a workspace location (where your projects will lie) and install the ADT plugin: click on **Help | Eclipse Marketplace...** and type **adt** (as shown in the following screenshot) in the textbox before pressing *Enter*; now select **Android Development Tools for Eclipse** by clicking on the **Install** button.

You don't have to select the NDK support feature, which provides support for Native Android Development (using the C or C++ language) since Spring For Android libraries are Java only libraries.

Installing the ADT plugin

Eclipse will prompt you several times about licenses and will eventually ask you to restart it.

1. When you're back in your workspace, make sure you have an (up-to-date) Android SDK installed on your machine: click on the icon with an Android robot coming out of a box, and install or update the Android SDK (you don't need all Android versions, you can just install the most popular ones such as 2.2 aka Froyo, 2.3.3 aka Gingerbread, 4.0.3 aka Ice Cream Sandwich and 4.1 aka Jelly Bean); restart Eclipse when you're done.

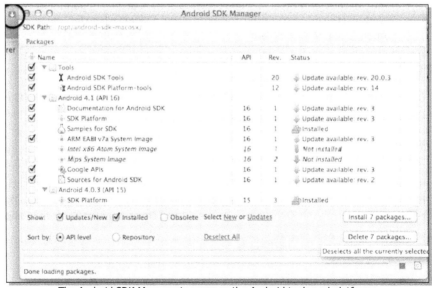

The Android SDK Manager to manage the Android tools and platforms

2. If you haven't done so already, you also need to create an **Android Virtual Device** (**AVD**) so that you can deploy your Android apps to it (you could also connect your phone or tablet via USB to deploy your apps on it); for that matter, click on the icon representing an Android robot in a device screen and create a new AVD, as shown in the following screenshot:

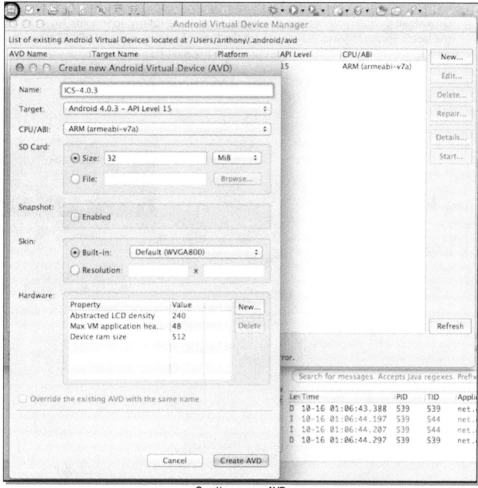

Creating a new AVD

You can find more details on the ADT plugin from the official website: `http://developer.android.com/tools/sdk/eclipse-adt.html`.

3. We finally need to download the Spring for Android JARs, go to the Spring for Android website: `http://www.springsource.org/spring-android` and click on the **Download** button (you can skip the registration in the following screen). Now choose the latest Spring for Android release (at the time of writing: 1.0.1.RELEASE) and unzip it on your machine; we will need the libraries in the next step:

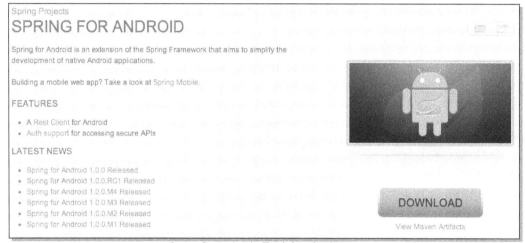

Spring for Android official download page

First example app

Now we are ready to create our first application with Spring for Android:

1. Click on **File | New... | Android Application,** give your project name and accept the defaults in the following dialogs:

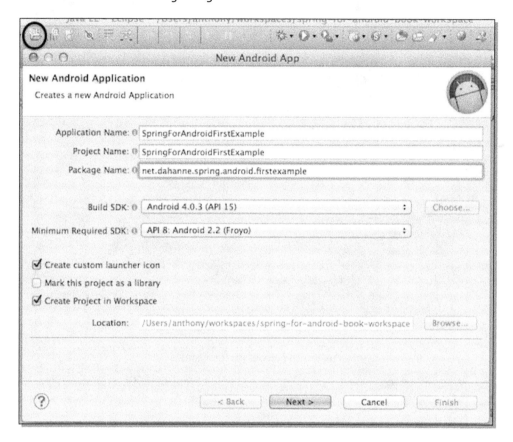

2. A new window named **New Android Application** will pop up, as shown in the following screenshot:

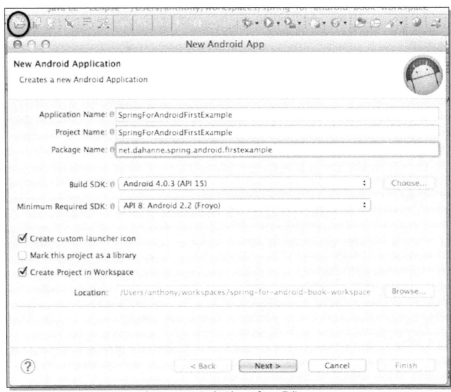

Creating an Android app from Eclipse

3. When asked for a new activity, choose the default **BlankActivity**, as shown in the following screenshot:

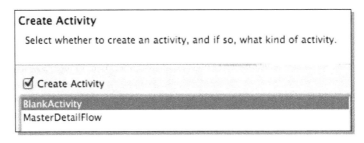

4. Now copy the JARs `spring-android-core-{version}.jar` and `spring-android-rest-template-{version}.jar` from the Spring for Android ZIP file you downloaded before, to the `$Project_home/libs` folder of your new project; you should have the following project structure:

First example app

5. For this first sample app to use Spring for Android to request a web service (we will use `http://ifconfig.me/all`), we will just need to perform a `GET` method on this URL and we will receive the client info: IP, User Agent, and so on. We will then need to declare our intention to access the network. This works by adding the following `permission` tag just before the `application` tag in the Android manifest file:

```
(...)<uses-sdk
        android:minSdkVersion="8"
        android:targetSdkVersion="15" />
<uses-permission android:name="android.permission.INTERNET"/>
<application (...)
```

The Android manifest is found at the root of the project: `AndroidManifest.xml`.

Forgetting to do so results in obscure messages in the log cat view (where all the logs are gathered) such as `Fatal Exception`; see `http://developer.android.com/guide/topics/security/permissions.html` for more information on permissions.

The HTTP protocol defines methods, or verbs, to indicate the action to be performed on the remote resource: `GET` to fetch a resource, `POST` to store a resource, `PUT` to update a resource, `DELETE` to delete a resource are examples of HTTP verbs, you can learn more about them by reading this article: `http://en.wikipedia.org/wiki/Hypertext_Transfer_Protocol`.

6. Then, we adjust the activity layout by removing the default "hello world" (`android:text="@string/hello_world"`) and replacing it by an anchor that we will use to print the response of the web service (`android:id="@+id/hello_text"`):

```
<RelativeLayout xmlns:android="http://schemas.android.com/apk/res/
android"
    xmlns:tools="http://schemas.android.com/tools"
    android:layout_width="match_parent"
    android:layout_height="match_parent" >
    <TextView
        android:id="@+id/result_text"
        android:layout_width="wrap_content"
        android:layout_height="wrap_content"
        android:layout_centerHorizontal="true"
        android:layout_centerVertical="true"
        tools:context=".MainActivity" />
</RelativeLayout>
```

The activity layout is found at `res/layout/activity_main.xml`.

7. Finally, we can rework `MainActivity` itself (only the `onCreate()` method needs to be updated):

```
@Override
public void onCreate(Bundle savedInstanceState) {
  super.onCreate(savedInstanceState);
  setContentView(R.layout.activity_main);
  final TextView resultTextView =
          (TextView) findViewById(R.id.result_text);
  AsyncTask<String, Void, String> simpleGetTask =
              new AsyncTask<String, Void, String>() {
```

```
@Override
protected String doInBackground(String... params) {
  //executed by a background thread

 //create a new RestTemplate instance
  RestTemplate restTemplate = new RestTemplate();

  //add the String message converter, since the result of
      // the call will be a String
  restTemplate.getMessageConverters().add(
            new StringHttpMessageConverter());

  // Make the HTTP GET request on the url (params[0]),
      // marshaling the response to a String
  return
        restTemplate.getForObject(params[0],String.class);
  }

  @Override
  protected void onPostExecute(String result) {
    // executed by the UI thread once the background
        // thread is done getting the result
    resultTextView.setText(result);
  }
};
String url = "http://ifconfig.me/all";
// triggers the task; it will update the resultTextView once
  // it is done
simpleGetTask.execute(url);
}
```

 If Eclipse complains about missing imports, press simultaneously *Shift + Ctrl + O* to automatically add the required the imports.

In this snippet, we first got a reference to our `result_text` text view, and set it to a `final` variable named `resultTextView` (`final` because we will need to access it through an inner class).

Next, we created an anonymous inner class, extending `AsyncTask` to implement all the logic of hitting the web service (creating the `RestTemplate` instance, adding the `String` converter and calling `getForObject`), and setting the result to the text view (using the `setText` method). When we call `simpleGetTask.execute(url)`, the URL is added to the array of params in `doInBackground(String... params)` (so `params[0]` is `url` in this case).

If we had directly written the code to hit the web service in the
onCreate() method, the application would not have even been able to
start since the Android platform prevents the developers from performing
HTTP requests in the UI (main) thread (and for a good reason: those
network-related operations often take time to complete, and would freeze
the UI while the operations were in progress).

```java
@Override
public void onCreate(Bundle savedInstanceState) {
 TextView resultTextView = (TextView) findViewById(R.id.result_
text);
 String url = "http://ifconfig.me/all";
 RestTemplate restTemplate = new RestTemplate();
 RestTemplate.getMessageConverters().add(new
StringHttpMessageConverter());
 String result = restTemplate.getForObject(url, String.class);
 resultTextView.setText(result);
}
```

 Do not do this! You can not perform HTTP-related calls
from the UI (main) thread.

 More information about AsyncTasks can be found in the official
documentation: http://developer.android.com/reference/android/
os/AsyncTask.html and also on threads and processes in Android in general:
http://developer.android.com/guide/components/processes-and-
threads.html.

8. We are now ready to launch this first Spring for Android based app!

   Right-click on the project name and select **Run as… | Android Application**:

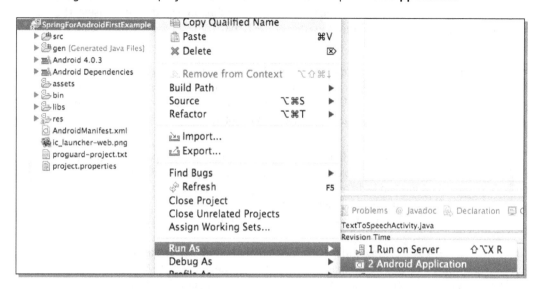

9. Eclipse will start your previously created AVD and will automatically run the app, you should see something similar to the following screenshot:

MainActivity screenshot from the AVD

Congratulations! You've successfully run your first Spring for Android based app!

Using Maven to build a Spring for Android app

In the previous example, we only added two JARs to the `libs` folder; but if you need other dependencies, such as `MessageConverters` (to unmarshall JSON, XML responses), the `Auth` module, or any other existing libraries in your project, managing your dependencies will soon become a burden!

Maven can help you manage your dependencies (in a nutshell, you specify them in a file called `pom.xml` and it will get them from the Internet automatically, including their transitive dependencies) and much more: release operations, tests runs, header generation, and so on. Maven is a modular open source build tool with tons of plugins!

 When using the Android Maven plugin, you should add to your environment the following variable `ANDROID_HOME` (linking your Android home directory) and add `ANDROID_HOME/platform-tools` to your path. This is explained in detailed in `https://code.google.com/p/maven-android-plugin/wiki/GettingStarted`.

To begin with, let's add the **m2e** (Maven to Eclipse) plugin to Eclipse: like we did for the ADT plugin, open **Help | Eclipse** Marketplace and search for **maven**; choose **Maven Integration for Eclipse**, click on **Install** and acknowledge the dialogs; restart your IDE at the end of the process.

Installing Maven Integration for Eclipse

Now import the project named `spring-for-android-first-example-maven` into your workspace: you can either clone it from GitHub or unzip the `examples.zip` archive; and then, from Eclipse, click on **File | Import...** and choose **Existing Maven Projects,** and click on **Next**.

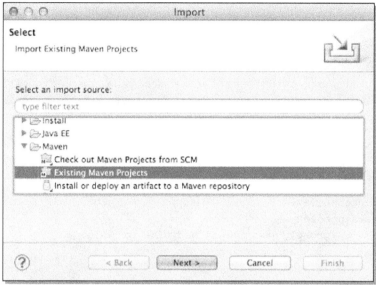

Import existing Maven project

Browse to the directory where you cloned or unzipped the project and click on the **Next** button:

Browse to your maven project

M2e will show you a list of m2e connectors needed to integrate the Maven-based project into your IDE (basically those connectors tell m2e how to generate and compile sources); click on **Finish** and accept the following dialogs; restart Eclipse.

 The most important connector here is the m2e-android connector : it enables m2e to integrate with ADT, more info on `http://rgladwell.github.com/m2e-android/`.

The project should be imported just fine and you can deploy the project on your AVD in the same way you did with the previous project (right-click on the project, and choose **Run as | Android application**).

Let's have a look though at the `pom.xml` file (the only additional file compared to the previous project), right-clicking on it and choosing **Open with... | Maven POM Editor**; click on the **pom.xml** tab at the bottom of the view.

```
(...)<dependencies>
        <dependency>
            <groupId>com.google.android</groupId>
            <artifactId>android</artifactId>
            <version>4.0.1.2</version>
            <scope>provided</scope>
        </dependency>
        <dependency>
          <groupId>org.springframework.android</groupId>
          <artifactId>spring-android-rest-template</artifactId>
          <version>${spring-android-version}</version>
        </dependency>
    </dependencies>
    <build>
        <finalName>${project.artifactId}</finalName>
        <sourceDirectory>src</sourceDirectory>
        <plugins>
            <plugin>
        <groupId>com.jayway.maven.plugins.android.generation2<//
groupId>
                <artifactId>android-maven-plugin</artifactId>
                <version>3.3.0</version>
                <extensions>true</extensions>
                <configuration>
                    <sdk>
                        <!-- platform or api level (api level 4 =
                            platform 1.6)-->
                        <platform>15</platform>
                    </sdk>
```

```
        </configuration>
      </plugin>
    </plugins>
  </build>(...)
```

There you can see in the dependencies section; the Android platform and the Spring for Android `RestTemplate` artifact (no need to specify Spring for Android core! Remember, Maven automatically gets the transitive dependencies) and in the plugins section the Android-Maven plugin (which extends Maven for Android projects, thanks to the `extensions=true` attribute), configured to require Android 4.0.3 (API level 15).

Maven at its core is a command-line tool, and if you download and unzip Maven on your machine, you could go to the root directory of the Maven project (where `pom.xml` resides) and type the Maven command with different goals:

✦ `mvn clean install`: To compile, run the tests and package

✦ `mvn clean install android:run`: To start your app in an AVD

To see all the available goals, you can type `mvn help:describe -Dplugin=com.jayway.maven.plugins.android. generation2:maven-android-plugin`.

You also can simulate command line Maven from inside Eclipse, right-clicking on the project and choosing **Run as | Maven build...**, and specifying your goals.

Maven installation instructions can be found online: `http://www. sonatype.com/books/mvnref-book/reference/installation-sect- maven-install.html`.

To learn more about Maven, I highly recommend to read the free and available online Maven book at `http://www.sonatype.com/books/ mvnref-book/reference/` which even has a specific Android chapter.

Now we are ready to hack together some richer Spring for Android based apps!

Quick start – RestTemplate

Now that our workspace is set up and we already successfully deployed our first Spring for Android `RestTemplate` based app, let's explore some more capabilities from `RestTemplate`.

This section relies on several example apps. We will go through all the important points of each code sample. Feel free to import the projects into your IDE and browse the code.

 From now on, I will use Maven to manage dependencies, but you don't have to. Each project has a list of dependencies in its `README.md` file: download them (or get them from your Spring for Android ZIP archive `libs` folder), and add them to the `libs` folder!

Different message converters

In the previous section, we already used a message converter: `StringHttpMessageConverter`. Each message converter supports reading from and writing to certain media types (often referred to as MIME types); `StringHttpMessageConverter` supports reading all kinds of documents (MIME */*) and writing to text (MIME text/plain). Let's discover more complex message converters.

 MIME (**Multipurpose Internet Mail Extensions**), is not only used to describe the content of e-mails, it is vastly used to describe the content of documents exchanged through HTTP as well (`http://en.wikipedia.org/wiki/MIME`).

MappingJacksonHttpMessageConverter

JSON messages are very frequent among REST web services. Originally designed for the JavaScript language (`JavaScriptObjectNotation`); they're lightweight and human readable as well.

`Ifconfig.me` can return a JSON response, if you use this URL : `http://ifconfig.me/all.json`.

In the code from our first example, let's replace `StringHttpMessageConverter` with `MappingJacksonHttpMessageConverter`:

```
AsyncTask<String, Void, IfConfigMeJson> simpleGetTask =
  new AsyncTask<String, Void, IfConfigMeJson>() {
  @Override
  protected IfConfigMeJson doInBackground(String... params) {
    String url = params[0];
    RestTemplate restTemplate = new RestTemplate();
```

```
    MappingJacksonHttpMessageConverter jacksonConverter =
        new MappingJacksonHttpMessageConverter();
    restTemplate.getMessageConverters().add(jacksonConverter);
    return restTemplate.getForObject(url,
        IfConfigMeJson.class);
  }


  @Override
  protected void onPostExecute(IfConfigMeJson result) {
    String resultAsString =  new StringBuilder()
                    .append("Your current IP is : ")
                    .append(result.getIpAddr()).toString();
    resultTextView.setText(resultAsString );
  }


};


String url = "http://ifconfig.me/all.json";
//triggers the task
simpleGetTask.execute(url);
```

As you can see, we also introduced a model class named IfConfigMeJson: this class
defines the mapping between the JSON messages properties ({"connection":"keep-
alive","ip_addr":"70.30.43.43", [..]}) and a **POJO** (**Plain Old Java Object**: a simple
class with member variables and their accessors), so that we can easily access each property of
the response (in the following example: result.getIpAddr()) in our Java code:

```
public class IfConfigMeJson {
  private String connection;
  @JsonProperty("ip_addr")
  private String ipAddr;
  public String getConnection() {
    return connection;
  }
  public void setConnection(String connection) {
    this.connection = connection;
  }
  public String getIpAddr() {
    return ipAddr;
  }
  public void setIpAddr(String opAddr) {
    this.ipAddr = opAddr;
  }
```

Jackson automatically matches JSON properties with Java fields as long as they are named identically (CamelCase in Java, underscore for JSON). You've certainly noticed that we mapped the JSON property `ip_addr` with the field `ipAddr`, to respect Java naming conventions, thanks to Jackson's `@JsonProperty` annotation before the field definition. On a side note, we could have declared the fields of the class as public and have the accessors removed.

When you run the application, you will only see the following screenshot:

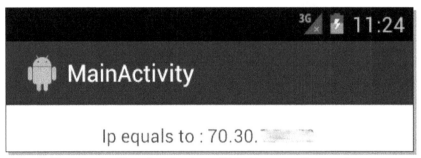

The app using `MappingJacksonHttpMessageConverter`

In this section we added a dependency to `jackson-mapper-asl` in our `pom.xml` file:

```
<dependency>
<groupId>org.codehaus.jackson</groupId>
  <artifactId>jackson-mapper-asl</artifactId>
  <version>${jackson-version}</version>
</dependency>
```

 There is another JSON message converter available, `GsonHttpMessageConverter`, using the Google Gson library instead of Jackson, that can be used alternatively.

SimpleXmlHttpMessageConverter

Another message converter worth mentioning is `SimpleXmlHttpMessageConverter`: it maps XML responses and requests to POJOs the same way `MappingJacksonHttpMessageConverter` did with JSON.

As an example, let's request the `Ifconfig.me` XML service: `http://ifconfig.me/all.xml`.

In the `MainActivity` class from our previous example, let's replace
`MappingJacksonHttpMessageConverter` with `SimpleXmlHttpMessageConverter`:

```
AsyncTask<String, Void, IfConfigMeXml> simpleGetTask =
    new AsyncTask<String, Void, IfConfigMeXml>() {
    @Override
    protected IfConfigMeXml doInBackground(String... params) {
        String url = params[0];
RestTemplate restTemplate = new RestTemplate();
        SimpleXmlHttpMessageConverter xmlConverter =
            new SimpleXmlHttpMessageConverter();
        restTemplate.getMessageConverters().add(xmlConverter);
        return restTemplate.getForObject(url, IfConfigMeXml.class);
    }

    @Override
    protected void onPostExecute(IfConfigMeXml result) {
        String resultAsString =  new StringBuilder()
                    .append("Your current IP is : ")
                    .append(result.getIpAddr()).toString();
        resultTextView.setText(resultAsString );
    }

};

    String url = "http://ifconfig.me/all.xml";
```

Once again, you'll notice we rely on a class, named `IfConfigMeXml.java`, to allow
`SimpleXml` to do the mapping between the XML response and the Java code. The following is
the XML response:

```
<info>
<forwarded/>
<ip_addr>70.43.43.43</ip_addr>
[...]
</info>
```

The following is the Java code:

```
@Root (name="info")
public class IfConfigMeXml {

  @Element(required=false)
  private String forwarded;

  @Element(name="ip_addr")
```

```
    private String ipAddr;
    [...]
}
```

The annotations are similar to the ones we used for the JSON message converter.

The `@Root` annotation defines what will be the name of the root XML tag: `info` in this case.

The `@Element` annotation is added before each field to let `SimpleXml` know those fields are mapped to XML tags: if `required` is set to false, it means the tag could be empty; if `name` is specified, it means the POJO field does not match the XML tag name.

If you run the application, you will get exactly the same output as we had in the previous example.

 In this section, we added a dependency to the `SimpleXml` framework. Unfortunately, this dependency has transitive dependencies to stax and xpp3 which are not needed for Android applications.

We had to explicitly filter some transitive dependencies to let Maven know not to add them to the classpath.

```xml
<dependency>
  <groupId>org.simpleframework</groupId>
  <artifactId>simple-xml</artifactId>
  <version>${simple-version}</version>
  <exclusions>
    <!-- StAX is not available on Android -->
    <exclusion>
      <artifactId>stax</artifactId>
      <groupId>stax</groupId>
    </exclusion>
    <exclusion>
      <artifactId>stax-api</artifactId>
      <groupId>stax</groupId>
    </exclusion>
    <!-- Provided by Android -->
    <exclusion>
      <artifactId>xpp3</artifactId>
      <groupId>xpp3</groupId>
    </exclusion>
  </exclusions>
</dependency>
```

RssChannelHttpMessageConverter

This message converter is about parsing RSS feeds; as usual we are going to inject it to our
`RestTemplate` instance, but this time we will read entries from a blog feed.

```
final WebView resultTextView = (WebView) findViewById(R.id.result_
text);
AsyncTask<String, Void, Channel> simpleGetTask =  new
AsyncTask<String, Void, Channel>() {
    @Override
    protected Channel doInBackground(String... params) {
        RestTemplate restTemplate = new RestTemplate();
        // Configure the RSS message converter.
        RssChannelHttpMessageConverter rssChannelConverter = new
RssChannelHttpMessageConverter();
        rssChannelConverter.setSupportedMediaTypes(
            Collections.singletonList(MediaType.TEXT_XML));

        // Add the RSS message converter to the RestTemplate instance
        restTemplate.getMessageConverters().add(rssChannelConverter);

        // Make the HTTP GET request on the url (params[0]), marshaling
//the response to a String
        return restTemplate.getForObject(params[0], Channel.class);
    }

    @Override
    protected void onPostExecute(Channel result) {
        //get the latest article from the blog
        Item item = (Item) result.getItems().get(0);

        // load the content of the article into the WebView
        resultTextView.loadData(item.getContent().getValue(), "text/
html", "UTF-8");
    }
};
String url = "http://blog.dahanne.net/feed/";
```

We don't have to create a POJO mapping class here since the result will always be a `Channel` –
a class providing us with methods to access the different property of the feed: items, language,
published date, and so on. In this example, we only read the content of the first item – the latest
article from my blog!

The feed looks as follows:

```xml
<?xml version="1.0" encoding="UTF-8"?>
<rss version="2.0">
<channel>
    <title>Anthony Dahanne&#039;s blog</title>
    <description>A blog</description>
    [...]
    <item>
        <title>Article 1</title>
        <description>content of the article</description>
        [...]
    </item>
    [...]
</channel>
</rss>
```

And the result on the device is as follows:

The content of the first item of an RSS feed

 You may have noticed that I switched the previous TextView for a WebView, capable of interpreting HTML code such as hyperlinks.

`RssChannelHttpMessageConverter` does not have default supported types, that's why we added the media type `text/xml` as a supported type.

We had to add a dependency on the Android ROME Feed Reader for this RSS feed example; this library is not published on Maven Central, which means we also had to declare the repository where its artifacts are deployed to.

```
<dependency>
    <groupId>com.google.code.android-rome-feed-reader</groupId>
    <artifactId>android-rome-feed-reader</artifactId>
    <version>${android-rome-version}</version>
</dependency>


<repositories>
    <repository>
        <id>android-rome-feed-reader-repository</id>
        <name>Android ROME Feed Reader Repository</name>
        <url>https://android-rome-feed-reader.googlecode.com/svn/maven2/releases</url>
    </repository>
</repositories>
```

Gzip encryption

To save bandwidth during transfers, as part of each request you can tell the server that you support gzip encryption. If the server supports gzipping the responses, it will do so.

Spring for Android `RestTemplate`, relies on Android `java.net.HttpURLConnection` since Gingerbread (2.3), which defaults in sending the `Accept-Encoding : gzip` header; so gzip compression is on by default.

Otherwise, you just need to specify in the headers of the request that you can support gzip. Let's have a look at a concrete example – the Jackson example where this time we only show the client supported encoding mechanism:

```
@Override
protected IfConfigMeJson doInBackground(String... params) {

    HttpHeaders requestHeaders = new HttpHeaders();
    requestHeaders.setAcceptEncoding(ContentCodingType.IDENTITY);
// Add the gzip Accept-Encoding header
//requestHeaders.setAcceptEncoding(ContentCodingType.GZIP);
    HttpEntity<?> requestEntity =
        new HttpEntity<Object>(requestHeaders);
    RestTemplate restTemplate = new RestTemplate();
```

```
MappingJacksonHttpMessageConverter jacksonConverter =
    new MappingJacksonHttpMessageConverter();
restTemplate.getMessageConverters().add(jacksonConverter);
ResponseEntity<IfConfigMeJson> response =
    restTemplate.exchange(params[0], HttpMethod.GET,
                requestEntity, IfConfigMeJson.class);
return response.getBody();
}
```

Using `Identity`, we declare that we do not support anything else other than raw text.

 When you ask for gzip explicitly or implicitly, `java.util.zip.GzipInputStream` will be automatically used to decode the response.

Did you notice that instead of using `getForObject(url, Pojo.class)` we used `exchange (url, GET, requestEntity, Pojo.class)`? The `exchange()` method is a more versatile method that allows for customization of the request.

Let's have a look at the request/response exchanged during the execution of this code:

Request (IDENTITY and then GZIP)	Response (IDENTITY and then GZIP)
GET/all.json HTTP/1.1	HTTP/1.1 200 OK
Accept: application/json	Date: Fri, 02 Nov 2012 02:41:04 GMT
Accept-Encoding: identity	
Content-Length: 0	Server: Apache
Host: ifconfig.me:80	Vary: Accept-Encoding
Connection: Keep-Alive	Connection: close
	Transfer-Encoding: chunked
	Content-Type: application/json
	13c
	{"connection":"Keep-Alive","ip_addr:[...],"encoding":"identity"}
	0

Request (IDENTITY and then GZIP)	Response (IDENTITY and then GZIP)
GET /all.json HTTP/1.1	HTTP/1.1 200 OK —îPq
Accept: application/json	Date: Fri, 02 Nov 2012 02:42:08 GMT
Accept-Encoding: gzip	Server: Apache
Content-Length: 0	Vary: Accept-Encoding
User-Agent: Dalvik/1.6.0 (Linux; U; Android 4.0.4; sdk Build/MR1)	Content-Encoding: gzip
	Content-Length: 258
Host: ifconfig.me:80	Connection: close
Connection: Keep-Alive	Content-Type: application/ json
X-Forwarded-For: 192.168.1.111	
	ã /%êAOÑO ÔÔ.
	"ì&À-
	"ß5fi'ãâg2€él●¥§4⊠˘ªÖΩÕ|3ÔeÊ˝
	2È"%9kgŸ/{&ö"ì—+±/"SáJ˘àk

It's often handy to analyze the requests and responses that go back and forth the device; you can use the open source software Membrane as an HTTP proxy (http://www.membrane-soa.org/soap-monitor/) creating a new simple proxy that listens to localhost:2000 and redirects to the web service you target (for example, http://ifconfig.me).

In the Android code, just replace your web service URL with computer_ip:2000 (could be 192.168.1.1:2000): you'll then see all the traffic between your Android app and the web service URL.

HTTP Basic authentication

This authentication scheme is, as its name implies it, very basic and unsecured. You just provide a username and a password to access a realm (usually a portion of a website).

As we did for the encoding, we can provide the credentials through a header: the username and the password will be Base64-encoded.

By no means does Base64 encoding provide security. You can decode it as easily as you encode it! See https://en.wikipedia.org/wiki/Base64 for more information on Base64.

As an example, we'll try to access a web page that displays **Hello World**; provided you sent the right credentials. The page is http://restfulapp.appspot.com/helloworld, and the credentials are username – s4a and password – s4a (you can try it in your web browser).

Let's try to access this page with Spring for Android's RestTemplate!

```
AsyncTask<String, Void, String> simpleGetTask =  new AsyncTask<String,
Void, String>() {
    @Override
    protected String doInBackground(String... params) {
        // Set the credentials for creating a Basic Auth request
        HttpAuthentication authHeader =
            new HttpBasicAuthentication("s4a", "s4a");
        HttpHeaders requestHeaders = new HttpHeaders();
        requestHeaders.setAuthorization(authHeader);
        HttpEntity<?> requestEntity =
            new HttpEntity<Object>(requestHeaders);

        RestTemplate restTemplate = new RestTemplate();

        restTemplate.getMessageConverters()
                .add(new StringHttpMessageConverter());

        try {
            // Make the GET request to the Basic Auth protected URL
            ResponseEntity<String> response =
                    restTemplate.exchange(params[0], HttpMethod.GET,
                        requestEntity, String.class);
            return response.getBody();
        } catch (HttpClientErrorException e) {
            // Handle 401 Unauthorized response
            Log.e("MainActivity",e.getLocalizedMessage(),e);
            return "Wrong credentials";
        }
    }

    @Override
    protected void onPostExecute(String result) {
        // executed by the UI thread
        resultTextView.setText(result);
    }

};
```

The way we set `Accepted-Encoding` in the previous example, we set an
HttpBasicAuthentication header to the `RestTemplate` headers.

Let's have a look at the request/response exchanged during the execution of this code:

Request	Response
GET/helloworld HTTP/1.1	HTTP/1.1 200 OK
Accept: text/plain, */*	Content-Type: text/plain; charset=iso-8859-1
Authorization: Basic czRhOnM0YQ==	
Content-Length: 0	Vary: Accept-Encoding
User-Agent: Dalvik/1.6.0 (Linux; U; Android 4.0.4; sdk Build/MR1)	Date: Fri, 02 Nov 2012 03:33:06
Host: restfulapp.appspot.com:80	Server: Google Frontend
Connection: Keep-Alive	Cache-Control: private
Accept-Encoding: gzip	Transfer-Encoding: chunked
	d
	Hello, world
	0

 The string `czRhOnM0YQ==` is the Base64 encoding of
`s4a:s4a`.

We will cover a better way to authenticate and also authorize a user and the user's app in the
next section: *Quick Start – OAuth*.

The RESTful recipe app

Let's study the case of the RESTful recipe app: an Android app to interact with a RESTful service
to create, update, read, and delete recipes.

A recipe is somewhat simple – it is a POJO with the following fields:

✦ An ID (`Integer`)

✦ A title (`String`)

✦ A description of the recipe (`String`)

✦ A type: usually an entree, a main dish or a dessert (`String`)

✦ An author (`String`)

The online web app that we will use as our backend service, is a JAX-RS (the JEE specification for REST services) application based on Jersey (the reference JAX-RS implementation library), and deployed on Google App Engine – it could have been written in Ruby, Python, or any other language.

 If you have already studied the Notepad app, part of the Android samples, you will be familiar with the RESTful recipe app: it was written using the Notepad App code as a base, replacing the persistence from an embedded SQLite database to a REST online service.

RecipeList activity: listing all recipes stored on the server

When the user launches the app, the first thing he wants to see is the list of the available recipes.

This activity uses `ListView`, backed with `ListAdapter` to display them to the user.

But first, it needs to get them from the server:

✦ We need a model (`Recipe.java`):

```
public class Recipe {

    private Long id;
    private String title;
    private String description;
    private String type;
    private String author;
}
```

✦ And a `RestTemplate` instance nested in an AsyncTask:

```
private class GetRecipesTask extends RecipeAbstractAsyncTask
<Void, Void, List<Recipe>> {

    @Override
    protected void onPreExecute() {
        showProgressDialog("Loading recipes. Please wait...");
    }

    @Override
    protected List<Recipe> doInBackground(Void... params) {
        HttpHeaders requestHeaders =
                prepareHeadersWithMediaTypeAndBasicAuthentication();

        // Populate the headers in an HttpEntity object
        HttpEntity<?> requestEntity =
```

```java
        new HttpEntity<Object>(requestHeaders);

    // Create a new RestTemplate instance
    RestTemplate restTemplate = new RestTemplate();
    restTemplate.getMessageConverters()
.add(new MappingJacksonHttpMessageConverter());

    try {
        // Perform the HTTP GET request
        ResponseEntity<Recipe[]> responseEntity =
            restTemplate.exchange(
                "http://www.restfulapp.appspot.com/rest/recipes/",
                HttpMethod.GET, requestEntity,
    Recipe[].class);
        return Arrays.asList(responseEntity.getBody());
    }
    catch (RestClientException e) {
        Log.e(TAG, e.getMessage(), e);
        exception = e;
        return null;
    }
}

@Override
protected void onPostExecute(List<Recipe> result) {
    dismissProgressDialog();
    if(result != null) {
        recipes = result;
    } else {
        String message = exception != null ?
            exception.getMessage() : "unknown reason";
        Toast.makeText(RecipesList.this,
            "A problem occurred during the reception of all
recipes
            : " +message , Toast.LENGTH_LONG).show();
         recipes = new ArrayList<Recipe>();
    }
    ListAdapter adapter = new RecipeAdapter(RecipesList.this,
        R.layout.recipeslist_item, recipes ) ;
    setListAdapter(adapter );
}
}
```

This task will get executed every time we need to get an updated list of recipes:

- ✦ When the activity is created (or resumed): `onResume()`
- ✦ When we're back from a successful update operation: `onActivityResult()`

You may have noticed that this AsyncTask extends `RecipeAbstractAsyncTask`, a class that defines an exception, and a utility method, `prepareHeadersWithMediaTypeAndBasicAuthentication()`:

```
protected HttpHeaders
prepareHeadersWithMediaTypeAndBasicAuthentication() {
      HttpHeaders requestHeaders = new HttpHeaders();
      List<MediaType> acceptableMediaTypes = new
ArrayList<MediaType>();
      acceptableMediaTypes.add(MediaType.APPLICATION_JSON);
      requestHeaders.setAccept(acceptableMediaTypes);
      HttpAuthentication authHeader = new
HttpBasicAuthentication("s4a", "s4a");
      requestHeaders.setAuthorization(authHeader);
      return requestHeaders;
   }
```

As its name implies, it prepares the request headers to include the Basic authentication needed, and the desired `MediaType` object from the server.

Back to `GetRecipesTask`: we prepare the request headers, we create a new `RestTemplate` instance – configured to use Jackson to (un)serialize the messages, and we perform the GET request:

```
// Perform the HTTP GET request
            ResponseEntity<Recipe[]> responseEntity = restTemplate.
exchange(getString(R.string.recipe_resource_url), HttpMethod.GET,
requestEntity, Recipe[].class);
```

The `R.string.resource_url` value is defined in `strings.xml` and is defined to be equal to: `http://www.restfulapp.appspot.com/rest/recipes/`.

Since we want to get a list of recipes, the type given to the `ResponseEntity` object is an array.

Another important thing to note is that the exception handler: **RestClientException** is, unlike its name, a wrapping server and client exception. If you want to tell your user what went wrong, you'd better catch this exception and keep it until you're back in the UI thread when executing the code in the `onPostExecute()` method.

Note that `RestClientException` is a subclass of `RuntimeException`, that's why you don't need to catch it explicitly. If you don't though, this exception could kill your activity if it is thrown.

Talking about the user interface, this task uses its pre-and post-execute methods to keep the user updated about the status of the loading by using `ProgresDialogs` and `Toasts`.

It can be useful to manually debug a REST resource, from outside your application; the **cURL** application (downloadable at `http://curl.haxx.se/download.html`) is probably the most popular tool to do so.

For each HTTP request evoked in this section, I will now include its matching cURL command line.

```
curl --user s4a:s4a  -H "Accept: application/json" -i http://www.
restfulapp.appspot.com/rest/recipes
[{"id":0,"title":"Montreal's Poutine","description":"French
fries are covered with fresh cheese curds, and topped with brown
gravy.","type":"MAIN_DISH","author":"Anthony"},{"id":1,"title":"a
title","description":"a description","type":"a type","author":"an
author"}]
```

An overview of the RecipesList activity

RecipeEditor activity

This activity is responsible for getting, updating, creating, and deleting the recipes.

The RecipeEditor activity in update mode

✦ GETting a recipe

When a user taps on the create icon of the RecipeList activity, or on one of the recipe title, he/she is directed to the RecipeEditor activity.

If the user wants to create a new recipe, he/she will see empty fields, but if he/she wants to see a recipe, they'll first get it from the server before filling the fields; thanks to the internal `GetRecipeTask`:

```
// Perform the HTTP GET request
Log.i(TAG,"Getting the recipe with id : "+params[0] + " : " +url +
params[0]);
ResponseEntity<Recipe> responseEntity = restTemplate.exchange(url
+ params[0], HttpMethod.GET, requestEntity,   Recipe.class);
return responseEntity.getBody();
```

Nothing really new here, we want to get a single recipe, identified by its ID (`params[0]`).

```
curl --user s4a:s4a  -H "Accept: application/json" -i http://www.
restfulapp.appspot.com/rest/recipes/0
{"id":0,"title":"Montreal's Poutine","description":"French fries
are covered with fresh cheese curds, and topped with brown
gravy.","type":"MAIN_DISH","author":"Anthony"}
```

◆ **PUTting a recipe**

To update one recipe, we must request the recipe resource with the PUT HTTP verb.

For that, we have, once again, a dedicated AsyncTask: UpdateRecipeTask, that will instantiate a RestTemplate instance, carrying the updated recipe (as soon as the user presses the Save button, we call the updateNote() method that syncs the content of the view, with the model of the current recipe).

```
// Create a new RestTemplate instance
RestTemplate restTemplate = new RestTemplate();
restTemplate.getMessageConverters()
    .add(new MappingJacksonHttpMessageConverter());

// Populate the headers in an HttpEntity object HttpEntity<Recipe>
requestEntity = new HttpEntity<Recipe>(recipe,requestHeaders);
try {
    // Perform the HTTP PUT request
    Log.i(TAG,"Updating the recipe with id : "
        +recipe.getId() + " : " + url);
    ResponseEntity<Void> responseEntity =
        restTemplate.exchange(url, HttpMethod.PUT, requestEntity,
        Void.class);
    if(responseEntity.getStatusCode() != HttpStatus.OK) {
        throw new HttpServerErrorException(
            responseEntity.getStatusCode());
    }
}
catch (RestClientException e) {
    Log.d(TAG, e.getMessage(), e);
    exception = e;
}
```

You can see the real important part here is RequestEntity, that wraps our recipe: RestTemplate will pass it along to Jackson that will convert it into a JSON string.

If the server does not respond with the HTTP Status 200 (OK), we can consider something went wrong and keep the exception for the user interface.

```
curl --user s4a:s4a  -H "Accept: application/json" -H "Content-
type: application/json"  -X PUT -d '{"id":"0", "title":"a
title","description":"a description","type":"a type","author":"an
author"}'  -i http://www.restfulapp.appspot.com/rest/recipes/
```

◆ **POSTing a recipe**

To create one recipe, we must request the recipe resource with the POST HTTP verb.

In the REST literature, you will also read about the usage of the PUT HTTP verb to create an entity too; but on one condition though – you would have to provide the ID (so that several PUT in a row do not change the resource state. PUT is idempotent just like GET and DELETE, and just as unsafe as DELETE and POST).

 In our case, we create a new resource, so POST reflects well our intention.

Let's have a look at `CreateRecipeTask`, which is very similar to `UpdateRecipeTask`:

```
// Populate the headers in an HttpEntity object
HttpEntity<Recipe> requestEntity =
    new HttpEntity<Recipe>(recipe,requestHeaders);
try {
    // Perform the HTTP POST request
    Log.i(TAG,"Posting the recipe with id : "
        +recipe.getId() + " : to " +url);
    ResponseEntity<Void> responseEntity =
        restTemplate.exchange(url, HttpMethod.POST,
requestEntity,
        Void.class);
    if(responseEntity.getStatusCode() != HttpStatus.CREATED) {
        throw new HttpServerErrorException(
            responseEntity.getStatusCode());
    }
}
catch (RestClientException e) {
    Log.d(TAG, e.getMessage(), e);
    exception = e;
}
return null;
```

Some interesting things to notice: the recipe does not have any ID set since the user is creating a recipe from nothing. The web service will assign an ID to this recipe (and should return the URI of the created resource); and the expected status is not 200, but 201 (`HttpStatus.CREATED`).

```
curl --user s4a:s4a  -H "Accept: application/json" -H
"Content-type: application/json"  -X POST -d '{"title":"a
title","description":"a description","type":"a type","author":"an
author"}'  -i http://www.restfulapp.appspot.com/rest/recipes/
```

✦ DELETing a recipe

To delete one recipe, we must request the recipe resource with the DELETE HTTP verb.

The AsyncTask named `DeleteRecipeTask` is similar to `GetRecipeTask` in the way that it only requires the ID of the recipe to be appended to the resource URI (there is no need to carry the whole recipe as we did with PUT and POST).

```
try {
    // Perform the HTTP DELETE request
    Log.i(TAG,"Deleting the recipe with id : "
        +recipe.getId() + " : from " +url +recipe.getId() );
    ResponseEntity<Void> responseEntity =
        restTemplate.exchange(url+recipe.getId(),
        HttpMethod.DELETE, requestEntity, Void.class);
    if(responseEntity.getStatusCode() != HttpStatus.NO_CONTENT) {
        throw new HttpServerErrorException(
        responseEntity.getStatusCode());
    }
}
catch (RestClientException e) {
    Log.d(TAG, e.getMessage(), e);
    exception = e;
}
```

This request expects to have a response with a 204 HTTP code, meaning the request was a success, but there is nothing to return (`HttpStatus.NO_CONTENT`).

HTTP code 200 would have been fine as a response to a successful DELETE request.

Check with your web service documentation (or better, experiment with cURL for example) to make the best assumptions about what is supposed to return a web service.

```
curl --user s4a:s4a  -H "Accept: application/json" -X DELETE    -i
http://www.restfulapp.appspot.com/rest/recipes/1
```

Android annotations

You may have heard about this project available at `https://github.com/excilys/androidannotations/` that aims at reducing the amount of code needed to inject views, activities, providers, services, and so on in an Android app.

The project leaders have decided to use Spring for Android's `RestTemplate` as the REST client library backing the REST annotations.

Android annotations is based on the **annotations processor tool (apt)**, now part of the Java 6 compiler; each annotated class will trigger the generation of a subclass (named the same with an _ appended to the filename, for example `OriginalActivity_.java`) that will contain all the boilerplate code the annotations saved you from writing!

So, along with `@Eactivity` (to allow an activity to use Android annotations), `@ViewById` (to inject your views), you have `@Get`, `@Post`, `@Put`, and so on.

Let's have a look at how we can benefit from Android annotations with the JSON example (getting the IP address from `Ifconfig.me`).

```
@EActivity(R.layout.activity_main)
public class MainActivity extends Activity {

    private IfConfigMeJson all;

    //inject the view to the activity layout
    @ViewById(R.id.result_text)
    TextView resultTextView;

    //inject the Rest service that wraps RestTemplate
    @RestService
    IfConfigMeRestClient restClient;
        //Use the Rest Service in a background thread
    @Background
    @AfterInject
    void getAllInfo() {
       all = restClient.getAll();
    }

    //wait a few seconds for the service to finish
    @UiThread(delay = 5000)
    @AfterViews
    void afterViews() {
       resultTextView.setText("Your IP is : "+all.getIpAddr());
    }

}
```

There is definitely less code, right?

You may have noticed though that we are using a new class named `IfConfigMeRestClient`:

```
@Rest(rootUrl = "http://ifconfig.me", converters =
        { MappingJacksonHttpMessageConverter.class })
public interface IfConfigMeRestClient {

    @Get("/all.json")
    @Accept(MediaType.APPLICATION_JSON)
    IfConfigMeJson getAll();

}
```

This class configures `RestTemplate` providing the converter class, the HTTP verb used, the mapping class (`IfConfigMeJson`), and the accepted media types.

Android annotations provides a good level of support to Spring for Android's `RestTemplate` (see `https://github.com/excilys/androidannotations/wiki/Rest-API` for the list of `RestTemplate` based annotations), and I suggest you try it to see if you prefer using it or not in your Spring for Android based project.

 If you start a project using Android annotations from scratch, I suggest you carefully follow those environment instructions: `https://github.com/excilys/androidannotations/wiki/Building-Project-Maven-Eclipse`.

Quick start – OAuth

OAuth is an open standard for authorization as Wikipedia puts it.

OAuth allows users to share their data or resources, hosted on a service provider, with websites or desktop or mobile apps.

Of course, if you gave your credentials (username and password) to those websites or apps, they could access your data on your behalf; but would you trust a third-party app or website to keep your credentials (your key to your digital life) safe? What if this app or website is malicious? Or simply unsecured? How many times have you read about a website getting its users credentials stolen, or keeping passwords in plain text in their databases?

OAuth is just about this; letting third-party apps or websites have a limited access (through a list of authorizations or scopes: `access user email`, `access user profile`, `can post messages on user behalf`, and so on) to your data, hosted on a service provider (the famous OAuth service providers are Google, Facebook, Twitter, Yahoo!, GitHub, LinkedIn, and so on) without ever giving them your credentials.

Developing a website or an app relying on a service provider

Have you ever noticed those **Login with Facebook** or **Login with Google** buttons on some websites (such as `Deezer.com`, `StackOverFlow.com`, and so on), or have you ever had a third-party Twitter app on an Android device (such as Twicca) request your Twitter credentials?

All those websites and apps use OAuth to get access to your data:

+ For one, they are saving you the trouble of having to create and remember yet other credential. They even enrich your user experience by accessing your data (such as your profile picture, activity info, and so on).

+ In addition, they gather a bigger audience (since the users don't have to go through the tedious account creation process) and they don't have to manage authentication credentials (with its risks) nor authorization.

Usually if a website or app creator wants to benefit from a service providing OAuth authorization, he/she has to register it against the OAuth service provider (Google, Facebook, and so on) which in turn will give him/her a **Client ID** and **Client secret** value:

Client ID for installed applications

Client ID:	508046100884-o6jgcn8e7c1g5gklhc8gibr80ouio8df.apps.googleusercontent.com
Client secret:	RuUyrF5qoGYWTFm1r_o8Gs4F
Redirect URIs:	urn:ietf:wg:oauth:2.0:oob
	http://localhost

Create another client ID...

Using the Google API Console to register a new application and associate it with a client ID and a client secret

Let's discover how this client ID and client secret enables the app to access the user's data.

The OAuth dance

An Android app (or any other installed app) relies on an OAuth 2.0 service provider such as Google. Let's have a look at the workflow of the OAuth authorization process in the following five simple steps:

1. The user launches the app for the first time; it will generate the token request – a URL to the service provider, including the app client ID and client secret, and also the several authorizations needed for the app (user info, userinfo e-mail, and so on).

   An example with Google OAuth 2.0 service provider:

   ```
   https://accounts.google.com/o/oauth2/auth?
   client_id=508046100884-o6jgcn8e7c1g5gklhc8gibr80ouio8df.apps.
   googleusercontent.com&
   response_type=code&
   redirect_uri=http://localhost&
   scope=https://www.googleapis.com/auth/userinfo.profile https://
   www.googleapis.com/auth/userinfo.email https://www.googleapis.com/
   auth/plus.me
   ```

2. This URL is loaded by the Android Chrome browser, most probably embedded in the app thanks to a WebView. The user is asked to accept or deny the authorizations asked by the app.

3. In return, if the user grants the app, the app will intercept the response from the embedded browser that contains an authorization code.

   An example of the response with Google OAuth 2.0 service provider:

   ```
   http://localhost/?code=4/urIB_wqrOqGpX-2w1UPXD8dHQAYO.
   ArEX_6EbNP0ZuJJVnL49Cc981fsNdgI
   ```

4. The app will finally exchange this authorization code for a token (if the lifetime of the token is limited, the app will also receive a refresh token and the expire time). This access token will be saved securely by the app.

An example of a token request/response with Google OAuth 2.0 service provider.

Request:

```
POST /o/oauth2/token HTTP/1.1
Host: accounts.google.com
Content-Type: application/x-www-form-urlencoded

code=4/v6xr77ewYqhvHSyW6UJ1w7jKwAzu&
client_id=8819981768.apps.googleusercontent.com&
client_secret={client_secret}&
redirect_uri=https://oauth2-login-demo.appspot.com/code&
grant_type=authorization_code
```

Response:

```
{
  "access_token":"1/fFAGRNJru1FTz70BzhT3Zg",
  "expires_in":3920,
  "token_type":"Bearer",
  "refresh_token":"1/xEoDL4iW3cxlI7yDbSRFYNG01kVKM2C-259HOF2aQbI"
}
```

5. The app will finally be able to interact with the resource (such as a REST service), provided it sends a valid token along with each of its requests.

An example of a request with a token with Google OAuth 2.0 service provider:

```
GET /oauth2/v1/userinfo HTTP/1.1
Authorization: Bearer 1/fFBGRNJru1FQd44AzqT3Zg
Host: googleapis.com
```

 Most, if not all, OAuth 2.0 service providers will only accept authorized service calls on HTTPS, to make sure the token can not be intercepted.

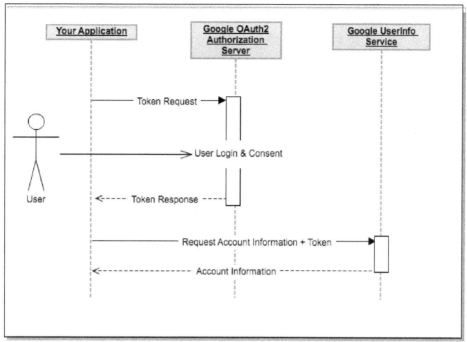

The OAuth workflow to access Google UserInfo Service, from `https://developers.google.com/accounts/docs/OAuth2`

You can read `https://developers.google.com/accounts/docs/OAuth2InstalledApp` to know the Google OAuth 2.0 service provider specifics, or `http://developers.facebook.com/docs/concepts/login/login-architecture/` to know about Facebook OAuth 2.0 service provider specifics.

It is strongly advised to read the OAuth service provider documentation before starting working on a client app (each of them have some subtle differences such as the parameters of the request token, the callback url, and so on).

Spring for Android Auth module

The Spring for Android `Auth` module supports both OAuth 1.0a and OAuth 2.0.

In a nutshell:

+ OAuth 2.0 allows for better support of non-webapps (such as an Android app)
+ OAuth 2.0 no longer requires developers to use cryptography
+ OAuth 2.0 access tokens are *short-lived* (thanks to the refresh tokens)

To know more about OAuth 2.0, you can read several articles from *Eran Hammer* on his blog: `http://hueniverse.com/2010/05/introducing-oauth-2-0/`

The Spring for Android `Auth` module depends on the following:

+ Spring for Android core (common classes: `Base64`, `StringUtils`, resource abstractions, and so on)

+ Spring for Android `RestTemplate` (REST API abstracting the underneath HttpClient)

+ Spring Social Core (OAuth 1.0 and 2.0 API wrapping the OAuth flows: request for authorization code, request for token, and so on)

+ Spring Security Crypto (provides support for symmetric encryption, key generation, and password encoding)

The `Auth` module itself defines cryptography and SQL classes for Android (to enable you to persist the authorization tokens securely to a SQLite Android database).

Spring for Android's `Auth` only contains seven classes as of now, that are about support for persisting OAuth tokens on an Android device; all the OAuth code is in Spring Social Core.

To make Twitter, Facebook, and Google apps developers' life easier, Spring Social has extensions, respectively named Spring Social Twitter, Spring Social Facebook, and Spring Social Google. These define APIs to access user's information, posts, contacts, agendas in each of those social networks.

An OAuth example using Google

We are going to build an Android app displaying information about a Google user: we are going to use Spring for Android `Auth` of course, but more importantly Spring Social and Spring Social Google.

The official documentation examples are about Facebook and Twitter. If you want to create an app interacting with those social networks, have a look at the Spring for Android examples at `https://github.com/SpringSource/spring-android-samples`.

Let's have a look at the `pom.xml` file of this project, in particular the inclusion of Spring Social Google:

```
<dependency>
  <groupId>org.springframework.social</groupId>
  <artifactId>spring-social-google</artifactId>
```

```
  <version>1.0.0.M1</version>
  <exclusions>
    <!-- Exclude in favor of Spring Android RestTemplate -->
    <exclusion>
      <artifactId>spring-web</artifactId>
      <groupId>org.springframework</groupId>
    </exclusion>
    <exclusion>
      <artifactId>spring-core</artifactId>
      <groupId>org.springframework</groupId>
    </exclusion>
  </exclusions>
</dependency>
[...]
<repository>
  <id>spring.social.google</id>
  <name>Spring Social Google</name>
  <url>https://github.com/GabiAxel/maven/raw/master/</url>
</repository>
```

You will notice here (in the `repository` section), this module is not hosted by Spring Source, because it is actually a community project not endorsed by Spring Source.

 This `pom.xml` file contains many exclusions; this is because most of the libraries used were developed with Java SE in mind, this is why they rely on Spring Core, Spring MVC, and so on. Spring for Android Core and `RestTemplate` provide the necessary dependencies for those modules.

Now let's have a look at the `AndroidManifest.xml` file:

```
[...]
<application
    android:name=".MainApplication"
    android:icon="@drawable/app_notes"
    android:label="@string/app_name" >
    <activity
        android:name=".GoogleActivity"
        android:label="@string/title_main" >
        [...]
    </activity>
    <activity
        android:name=".GoogleWebOAuthActivity"
        android:excludeFromRecents="true"
        android:noHistory="true" />
```

```
        <activity android:name=".GoogleProfileActivity" />
    </application>
```

For the first time in our examples, we are going to use an `Application` class, named here `MainApplication`.

 `GoogleWebOAuthActivity` will embed a browser and will only be launched for authentication. We don't want this activity to be part of the app history or the user to be able to get back to it; that's why we added `android:noHistory="true"` and `android:excludeFromRecents="true"`. More info on this is available at `http://developer.android.com/guide/topics/manifest/activity-element.html`.

This class will be used to prepare the two most important factories of our app (they will be accessed in all the activities): `ConnectionFactoryRegistry` and `ConnectionRepository`:

```
public class MainApplication extends Application {
  private ConnectionFactoryRegistry connectionFactoryRegistry;
  private SQLiteOpenHelper repositoryHelper;
  private ConnectionRepository connectionRepository;

  // **************************************
  // Application Methods
  // **************************************
  @Override
  public void onCreate() {
    // create a new ConnectionFactoryLocator and populate it with
Google ConnectionFactory
    this.connectionFactoryRegistry = new ConnectionFactoryRegistry();
    this.connectionFactoryRegistry.addConnectionFactory(new GoogleConn
ectionFactory(getClientId(),
      getClientSecret()));

    // set up the database and encryption
    this.repositoryHelper - new SQLiteConnectionRepositoryHelper(th
is);
    this.connectionRepository = new SQLiteConnectionRepository(this.
repositoryHelper,
      this.connectionFactoryRegistry, AndroidEncryptors.
text("password", "5c0744940b5c369b"));
  }
```

As you can see, in the `onCreate()` method we initialize:

- ✦ `ConnectionFactoryRegistry`: With the client ID and the client secret of the application from `ConnectionFactoryRegistry`, we'll have access to `GoogleConnectionFactory` which is the Google services extension of `OAuth2ConnectionFactory` that gives access to all OAuth operations

- ✦ `ConnectionRepository`: This will be responsible for persisting `ConnectionFactoryRegistry`, so that the OAuth token can be retrieved without needing to do the whole OAuth workflow every time

You may have noticed the use of a salt and a password (encryption) during the initialization of the database.

This will prevent a malicious app from being able to access the device database to retrieve the user OAuth token. A brief reminder: the app will never have access to the user's Google password. The authentication to the service provider, Google in this example, is always performed from the device browser.

Let's have a look at the main activity of that project, `GoogleActivity` that will be launched at startup:

```
@Override
public void onStart() {
  super.onStart();
  if (isConnected()) {
    showGoogleOptions();
  } else {
    showConnectOption();
  }
}


private boolean isConnected() {
  return connectionRepository.findPrimaryConnection(Google.class) !=
null;
}
```

This activity will display a list of entries related to the user profile if he/she is connected or just a **Connect** button if the user is not connected yet (since `GoogleConnectionFactoryRegistry` is persisted in a database, just looking up a connection of type `Google` in `ConnectionRepository` is enough to know whether or not the access token is already fetched).

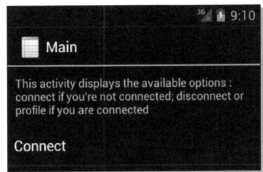

The GoogleActivity if the user has not yet logged in

So, in the case that we are not connected, taping on **Connect** will call `displayGoogleAuthorization()` which will launch `GoogleWebOAuthActivity`.

`GoogleWebOAuthActivity` is certainly the most important activity of this app. It is responsible for the OAuth 2.0 authentication and authorization.

```java
@Override
public void onCreate(Bundle savedInstanceState) {
  super.onCreate(savedInstanceState);

  //javascript is mandatory
  getWebView().getSettings().setJavaScriptEnabled(true);

  // Using a custom web view client to capture the access token
  getWebView().setWebViewClient(new GoogleOAuthWebViewClient());

  this.connectionRepository = getApplicationContext().
getConnectionRepository();
  this.connectionFactory = getApplicationContext().
getGoogleConnectionFactory();
}

@Override
public void onStart() {
  super.onStart();

  // display the Google authorization page
  getWebView().loadUrl(getAuthorizeUrl());
```

```
}

// *************************************
// Private methods
// *************************************
private String getAuthorizeUrl() {
  String redirectUri = getString(R.string.google_oauth_callback_url);
  String scope = getString(R.string.google_scope);

  // Generate the Google authorization url to be used in the browser
  OAuth2Parameters params = new OAuth2Parameters();
  params.setRedirectUri(redirectUri);
  params.setScope(scope);
  return this.connectionFactory.getOAuthOperations().
buildAuthorizeUrl(GrantType.AUTHORIZATION_CODE, params);
}
```

When this activity is created, it configures the associated WebView (you will notice this activity extends `AbstractWebViewActivity` that injects a Chrome Browser instance into a WebView) to accept JavaScript (the service provider and Google OAuth 2.0 requires JavaScript to authenticate the user) and injects a custom `WebViewClient` object that we will use to intercept OAuth flows (more on that in a moment).

Then, when the activity starts, we ask the WebView (the embedded Chrome browser) to request the authorization code for this app (see step 1 of *The OAuth dance* section).

This request is built using a callback URL, the scope of the authorizations needed for the app, and the client ID and secret (those two were already given to Spring OAuth when we created `ConnectionFactoryRegistry`).

```
<resources>
    <string name="google_app_id">508046100884-
o6jgcn8e7c1g5gklhc8gibr80ouio8df.apps.googleusercontent.com</string>
    <string name="google_app_secret">RuUyrF5qoGYWTFm1r_o8Gs4F</string>
    <string name="google_oauth_callback_url">http://localhost</string>
    <string name="google_scope">https://www.googleapis.com/auth/
userinfo.profile https://www.googleapis.com/auth/userinfo.email
https://www.googleapis.com/auth/plus.me</string>
</resources>
```

The callback URL here is `http://localhost`, because Google OAuth 2.0 service provider gives the choice between `http://localhost` and `urn:ietf:wg:oauth:2.0:oob`.

This will impact the response holding the authorization code; whether it will be part of a query string parameter or in the title bar of the browser. You can read `https://developers.google.com/accounts/docs/OAuth2Insta lledApp#choosingredirecturi` for more details.

If the user has not yet authenticated to any Google web services from his device, he/she should see a dialog inviting him/her to authenticate:

This dialog only appears if the user has not yet been authenticated to any Google services on his device

In all cases though, the user will see this authorization dialog which lists all the *scopes* the app has requested:

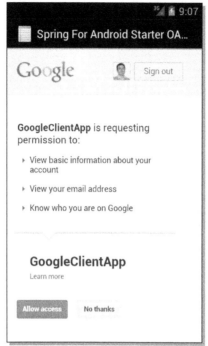

Google OAuth 2.0 service provider authorization dialog

 If the user denies the authorization, then, as expected, the authorization process will be terminated.

According to the service provider, this dialog may vary.

Once the user accepts the requested authorizations, GoogleWebOAuthActivity will detect that the web client is being redirected to a localhost (**the callback URI**), with the authorization code:

```
private class GoogleOAuthWebViewClient extends WebViewClient {

    private static final String LOCALHOST = "localhost";
    private static final String CODE = "code";

    /*
    * The WebViewClient has another method called
shouldOverridUrlLoading which does not capture the javascript
    * redirect to the success page. So we're using onPageStarted to
capture the url.
```

```
    */
   @Override
   public void onPageStarted(WebView view, String url, Bitmap favicon)
{
    // parse the captured url
    Uri uri = Uri.parse(url);
     // log the url : very interesting for debugging the OAuth
workflow
    Log.d(TAG, url);

    /*
     * The WebViewClient is launched to load an URL from the provider
that will ask the user whether or not he accepts our app to access his
data.
     * Once the provider successfully gets the approval from the user,
it will redirect this WebViewClient to the callback_uri, with a query
parameter named "code" : this is the authorization code
     */
    String host = uri.getHost();
    String code = uri.getQueryParameter(CODE);


    // The WebViewClient is redirected to the callback_uri, let's
trade the authorization code for the access token
    if (LOCALHOST.equals(host)) {
      if(!exchangeAuthorizationCodeForAccessToken.getStatus().
equals(AsyncTask.Status.RUNNING)) {
        exchangeAuthorizationCodeForAccessToken.execute(code);
        Toast.makeText(getApplicationContext(), "Redirecting you to
the app main activity", Toast.LENGTH_LONG).show();
        //preparing to quit this activity for the main activity
        getWebView().setVisibility(View.INVISIBLE);
      }
    }
  }
}
```

`exchangeAuthorizationCodeForAccessToken.execute(code)` will execute the following AsyncTask (we are going to send back the authorization code from our app, using `RestTemplate`, relying on Java `UrlConnection`, so we need to code this call from a background thread):

```
private AsyncTask<String, Void, Void>
exchangeAuthorizationCodeForAccessToken =  new AsyncTask<String, Void,
Void>() {
```

```
    private Exception exception;

    @Override
    protected Void doInBackground(String... params) {
      // executed by a background thread
      //params[0] should contain the authorization code
      try {
        AccessGrant exchangeForAccess = connectionFactory.
getOAuthOperations().exchangeForAccess(params[0], getString(R.string.
google_oauth_callback_url), null);
        Connection<Google> connection = connectionFactory.createConnecti
on(exchangeForAccess);
        connectionRepository.addConnection(connection);
      } catch (DuplicateConnectionException e) {
        Log.e(TAG,"something went wrong when adding the accessToken to
the connection repository",e);
        exception = e;
      } catch (Exception e) {
        Log.e(TAG,"something went wrong when adding the accessToken to
the connection repository",e);
        exception = e;
      }
      return null;
    }


    @Override
    protected void onPostExecute(Void result) {
      // executed by the UI thread once the background thread is done
getting the result
      if(exception != null) {
        Toast.makeText(getApplicationContext(), exception.getMessage(),
Toast.LENGTH_LONG).show();
      }
      // we go back to the main activity to display the options
      displayGoogleOptions();
    }

  };
```

Once the exchangeForAccess method is called, we retrieve the user token and we persist it in the ConnectionRepository class.

Our app is finally authorized to access the user's Google profile!

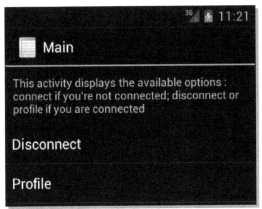

The GoogleActivity if the user has not yet logged in

If the user clicks on **Profile**, he will launch `GoogleProfileActivity`, from which, as you may expect, we get the user profile.

To do so we are using an AsyncTask, named `FetchProfileTask`, that will hit two Google web services: `UserOperations` (to read the main profile of the user and his/her profile picture) and `PersonOperations` (to read his/her Google+ profile, here we will just access the **about me** description):

```
@Override
protected LegacyGoogleProfile doInBackground(Void... params) {

    LegacyGoogleProfile userProfile = google.userOperations().
getUserProfile();
    aboutMe = google.personOperations().getGoogleProfile().
getAboutMe();
    profileBitmap = BitmapFactory.decodeStream(new URL(userProfile.
getProfilePictureUrl()).openConnection().getInputStream());
    return userProfile;

}
```

This information is then injected into the view:

The GoogleProfileActivity displaying the user profile picture, "about me" description and some profile info

People and places you should get to know

If you need help with Spring for Android (or REST or OAuth in general), the following are some people and places which will prove invaluable.

Official sites

✦ Homepage: `http://www.springsource.org/spring-android`

✦ Manual and documentation: `http://static.springsource.org/spring-android/docs/1.0.x/reference/htmlsingle/`

✦ Blog: `http://blog.springsource.org/category/android/`

✦ Source code: `https://github.com/SpringSource/spring-android`

✦ Official example's source code: `https://github.com/SpringSource/spring-android-samples`

✦ Android Maven Plugin: `http://code.google.com/p/maven-android-plugin/`

Articles and tutorials

✦ Explanation of OAuth: `http://hueniverse.com/oauth/guide/`

✦ OAuth for Google services: `http://support.google.com/a/bin/answer.py?hl=en&answer=61017`

✦ Official Android documentation about remote connections: `http://developer.android.com/training/basics/network-ops/connecting.html`

Community

✦ Official forums: `http://forum.springsource.org/forumdisplay.php?88-Android`

✦ Official bug tracker: `https://jira.springsource.org/browse/ANDROID`

Blogs

✦ Android team blog: `http://android-developers.blogspot.ca/`

Twitter

✦ Follow Spring for Android on Twitter: `https://twitter.com/springandroid`

✦ Follow Roy Clarkson (Spring for Android lead developer) on Twitter: `https://twitter.com/royclarkson`

✦ For more Open Source information, follow Packt at: `http://twitter.com/#!/packtopensource`

About Packt Publishing

Packt, pronounced 'packed', published its first book *"Mastering phpMyAdmin for Effective MySQL Management"* in April 2004 and subsequently continued to specialize in publishing highly focused books on specific technologies and solutions.

Our books and publications share the experiences of your fellow IT professionals in adapting and customizing today's systems, applications, and frameworks. Our solution based books give you the knowledge and power to customize the software and technologies you're using to get the job done. Packt books are more specific and less general than the IT books you have seen in the past. Our unique business model allows us to bring you more focused information, giving you more of what you need to know, and less of what you don't.

Packt is a modern, yet unique publishing company, which focuses on producing quality, cutting-edge books for communities of developers, administrators, and newbies alike. For more information, please visit our website: www.packtpub.com.

Writing for Packt

We welcome all inquiries from people who are interested in authoring. Book proposals should be sent to author@packtpub.com. If your book idea is still at an early stage and you would like to discuss it first before writing a formal book proposal, contact us; one of our commissioning editors will get in touch with you.

We're not just looking for published authors; if you have strong technical skills but no writing experience, our experienced editors can help you develop a writing career, or simply get some additional reward for your expertise.

Spring Security 3.1

ISBN: 978-1-84951-826-0   Paperback: 456 pages

Secure your web applications from hackers with this step-by-step guide

1. Learn to leverage the power of Spring Security to keep intruders at bay through simple examples that illustrate real world problems

2. Each sample demonstrates key concepts allowing you to build your knowledge of the architecture in a practical and incremental way

3. Filled with samples that clearly illustrate how to integrate with the technologies and frameworks of your choice

Learning Vaadin

ISBN: 978-1-84951-522-1   Paperback: 412 pages

Master the full range of web development features powered by Vaadin-built RIAs

1. Discover the Vaadin framework in a progressive and structured way

2. Create outstanding new components by yourself

3. Integrate with your existing frameworks and infrastructure

Please check **www.PacktPub.com** for information on our titles

Spring Data

ISBN: 978-1-84951-904-5   Paperback: 160 pages

Implement JPA repositories with less code and harness the performance of Redis in your applications

1. Implement JPA repositories with lesser code

2. Includes functional sample projects that demonstrate the described concepts in action and help you start experimenting right away

3. Provides step-by-step instructions and a lot of code examples that are easy to follow and help you to get started from page one

JasperReports 3.5 for Java Developers

ISBN: 978-1-84719-808-2   Paperback: 368 pages

Create, Design, Format, and Export Reports with the world's most popular Java reporting library

1. Create better, smarter, and more professional reports using comprehensive and proven methods

2. Group scattered data into meaningful reports, and make the reports appealing by adding charts and graphics

3. Discover techniques to integrate with Hibernate, Spring, JSF, and Struts, and to export to different file formats

Please check **www.PacktPub.com** for information on our titles